blur

an illustrated biography *by Linda Holorny*

⬤ **OMNIBUS PRESS**
LONDON / NEW YORK / PARIS / SYDNEY

Copyright © 1995 Omnibus Press.

(A Division of Book Sales Limited)

Edited by Chris Charlesworth.

Cover & book designed by Michael Bell Design.

Picture research by Nikki Russell.

ISBN 0.7119.5044.X

Order No. OP47777

Exclusive Distributors:

Book Sales Limited

8/9 Frith Street, London W1V 5TZ, UK.

Music Sales Corporation

257 Park Avenue South, New York, NY 10010, USA.

Music Sales Pty Limited

120 Rothschild Avenue, Rosebery, NSW 2018, Australia.

To the Music Trade only:

Music Sales Limited

8/9 Frith Street, London W1V 5TZ, UK.

Photo credits:

All Action: 2,12,16,34b,38,43t,45t&b; Peter Anderson/SIN: 1,28,30,32,35;

Matt Anker/Retna: 5, Colin Bell/Retna: 7; Jeff Davy/Retna: 29l; Steve Double/

Retna: front cover,3,17,18,23,26,41; Patrick Ford/Redferns: 37l;

Martin Goodacre/SIN: 21b; Steve Gillett/Redferns: 37r; Karl Grant/Retna: 24, 25;

Adrian Green/Retna: 39; Liane Hentscher/SIN: 20; Alastair Indge/Retna:

8,13,19,21t,22l&r; London Features International: back cover,4,9,10,11,14,15,

33,36,43b,44,47; Ilpo Musto/Rex Features: 34t; Valerie Phillips/Retna: 29r;

Steve Pyke/Retna: 40,42; Brian Rasic/Rex Features: 31t; Ed Sirrs/Retna: 31b;

Paul Slattery/Retna: 27; Barbara Steinwehe/Redferns: 6.

Every effort has been made to trace the copyright holders
of the photographs in this book but one or two were unreachable.
We would be grateful if the photographers concerned would contact us.

A catalogue record for this book is available from the British Library.

Grateful thanks to Hilary Donlon for additional research.

Printed in the United Kingdom by
J.B. Offset Printers (Marks Tey) Limited,
Marks Tey, Colchester, Essex.

"When our third album comes out our position as the quintessential English band of the Nineties will be assured. That is a simple statement of fact."

So said Damon Albarn, lead singer with Blur, in 1990, when his band's début album had just punctured the national charts at No.7 and their four faces were festooned across the serious music press and teenybop magazines alike. Who would have bet against him at that point? In just a matter of months Blur had appeared from almost nowhere to occupy a place alongside credibility giants The Stone Roses and bubblegum squeak Jason Donovan. But those betting on his optimism would not have been so enthusiastic eighteen months later, when Blur staggered on to the stage at London's Town and Country club, hopelessly drunk, musically shambolic and with their shattered morale at an all-time low. Yet, two years down the line and Damon Albarn's prediction seemed spot on, as Blur sat on the throne of Brit pop, crowned masters of their own genre with an album of such individuality and refreshingly stubborn awkwardness, that the entire musical community had been forced to doff its collective hat.

Graham Coxon was born in a military hospital in Rinteln, near Hanover in the old West Germany, to an army bandsman father, who taught jazz at Saturday morning classes. His army family childhood was typically itinerant, starting at the German military base for five years, then moving to Derby to live with his grandfather, then on to Colchester three years later. It wasn't until he attended Stanway Comprehensive School at the turn of the Eighties that Graham began to immerse himself in the music around him. His first loves were Two Tone and The Jam, and soon after he taught himself to play the saxophone and the guitar, both with creditable ease. As ever, there were like-minded kids at school who came together through shared tastes in music and fashion, and in this manner 14-year-old-Graham befriended an unusual character called Damon Albarn. Their fascination with music was mutual, and while the other boys ran over to the football pitch, Damon and Graham went behind the music block and talked bands. Soon after, they both went on holiday with Graham's parents, cementing an already close friendship which would go on to form the foundation for the success of Blur.

A school year older than his friend Graham, Damon Albarn's family background was rather more colourful. His father had been an associate of Sixties jazz rock experimentalists The Soft Machine, who featured the highly talented Robert Wyatt on drums and vocals. Albarn Senior was trained as an artist and constructed many conceptual stage designs for events known as 'happenings', such as the so-called 'Discotheque Interplay' built on a beach in southern France in 1967.

When Damon was born in Whitechapel Hospital, East London, in March 1968, the Albarns were living in a Victorian house in leafy Leytonstone, where they were the proud owners of some strange plastic chairs which Cat Stevens had given to Damon's father when the singer embraced Islam and renounced all his worldly goods in the mid-Seventies. Damon's room was filled with the fossils and the stuffed animals that he collected, and despite growing up in a Bohemian atmosphere he showed little interest in drinking, smoking or free sex. Even in 1978, when Damon lived in Turkey for three months, he abstained from mindless enjoyment, which suited his next home in Colchester, the capital of Essex rock'n'roll.

Damon's father had been offered a job running an art school, so the Albarns re-located once more, this time to a 14th century four bedroom house. Up until now, Damon had been into "football and girls and fossils", but with the start of the Eighties his attention suddenly turned to music and drama. Initially his musical obsession was classical. He adored pieces such as Vaughan Williams' 'The Lark Ascending' and as an aspiring pianist he proved to be an adept composer, a talent recognised when a score he wrote won a heat in the 'Young Composer of the Year Awards'. After a brief flirtation with Motown, Damon became immersed in Two Tone, the peculiarly British twist on Jamaican ska that was captivating his school mates. Pretty soon his school books were disfigured with the monochrome dancing man logos of Madness and The Specials, and as his tastes expanded, he discovered The Jam, The Kinks and other English gems, even the glories of Adam and The Ants, whom he called "the full stop after punk". Even so, he remained faithful to classical music, and to this day maintains that writing for ensembles, and his experiences in orchestras, were vital to his development. Indeed, he revealed in 1994 that the 3/4 material he would later write for Blur was all related to this classical interest, and that, more specifically, "Weill and Brecht's 'Die Drei Groschen Oper' *(The Threepenny Opera)* had more influence on me than any pop record."

Despite his natural ability with music, Damon failed his 'A' level music exam, and headed instead for a strict method acting school called East 15, where he was obliged to act out various roles including the Ayatollah Khomeini, a tramp and a female secretary. Unsurprisingly, he didn't take to this bizarre acting approach and, convinced he was not good enough, moved to London and art school. It was a time for hedonism. One story he tells of these drinking days is waking up at 5am in Holborn Police Station sitting next to a Gurkha. While he was mingling with art school types, (including morbid surrealist Damien Hirst of Farmyard fame) Damon is alleged to have formed a highly embarrassing soul pop duo named Two's A Crowd, and performed as a mime artist in make-up. Whether out of belief in his musical talent, or in an attempt to save him from soul pop hell, Damon's grandfather lent the youngster £3,000 to make his own demo. By this stage, Damon worked as studio teaboy at the Beat Factory Studios in Euston and at Le Croissant in Euston station by day, while by night he honed his musical compositions at the studio. Here he played around with various weird styles, including piano-only monstrosities with no vocals, but even so managed to produce early crude versions of several Blur songs, including the excellent 'Birthday'.

While Damon attended the bizarre method acting school, Graham left the Comprehensive
and headed for Colchester Art College. Then, when his friend moved to London, Graham moved
to Goldsmiths' College in New Cross where at 19 he enrolled on a Fine Arts Degree Course. He
continued to follow music and counted among his most prized possessions a noose that Morrissey
had thrown into the crowd at a Smiths gig. The two friends remained in daily contact: Damon had
become a surrogate music student by joining a part-time course at Goldsmiths' as well, "just
to get on campus", and he often played Graham his strange studio compositions. Brimming with
confidence, Damon recorded a demo on which Graham played saxophone and drums, and booked
solo gigs which Graham attended. Damon later said of their musical partnership that he and
Graham were "a Jam fanatic who couldn't play saxophone and a bad actor into Kurt Weill and
American theatre, the Forties and Fifties musicals". Once Damon had his tape ready he took it to
various record company types, including Dave Ambrose at EMI, who had signed The Sex Pistols
and Duran Duran among others. Damon performed to a backing tape in his office, Ambrose listened
politely then mumbled something about David Bowie and The House of Love and closed the door.

In the meantime Graham had met another musical friend called Alex James, who was studying French at the College. Alex was two months older than Damon and had been brought up in Bournemouth by a father who sold fork-lift trucks and a mother who did voluntary work, including the local Books On Wheels service. At the age of 11, Alex bought a piano for £100 and he also studied violin. At school he was academically brilliant, passing all his exams with flying colours, and he even played a few games for Southampton F.C.'s reserve team, but his real interest lay in music. He named his first band, Mr. Pang's Big Bangs, after his landlord, and soon after went to Goldsmiths' College to widen his artistic horizons. Along with Graham, Alex delved into art and artistic movements, including their own brand called 'Nichtkunst'. Then Graham introduced Alex to Damon as a potential bassist. The Bournemouth student's first impression of the future Blur front man was very clear: "He completely pissed me off."

The final piece of the jigsaw fitted into place when Dave Rowntree was recruited as drummer. Dave had played with Graham in various shabby groups in Colchester, the most worthy of which was Idle Vice. Dave was five years older than the others, and appeared to be relatively settled as a computer engineer. However, his musical ear came from both his Dad, who had commuted for 40 years to his job as a BBC sound engineer, and his mother, who had played in the London Orchestra. The young Dave had been taught to play drums the hard way – by a gargantuan Scotsman who taped a sixpence to the drum skin and smacked the pupil across the back of the head if his stick ever missed the target. By coincidence, Dave had also attended some of the Saturday morning jazz classes run by Damon's father.

Not as academically talented as Alex, Dave studied for a HND in Computer Science at Woolwich, then moved back to Colchester and began involving himself in bands. While he had played in Idle Vice with Graham, Dave had also been in his own band called Hazel Dean and The Carp Eaters From Hell. He became a protest vegetarian, but failed to adhere to basic nutritional requirements and wound up in hospital suffering from malnutrition. He also lived in London for three months as a squat punk with a mohawk and played at various squat gigs around King's Cross, after which he moved wholesale to France and made a meagre living busking and playing in small-time clubs. On returning to the UK, he managed to get a job as the local council's computer programmer, complete with a suit and a mohawk. By now it had lost its fluorescent punk look and turned black.

Blur have always been an awkward band, something of a misnomer in an industry that demands compatibility. There has always been a deal of confusion about their music and philosophy, and the band's formation is shrouded in mystery and uncertainty. There are several theories as to how they finally crystallised as a unit, and in a tradition that suggests a deep understanding of the value of mystery in pop, no-one seems willing to offer a definitive account. What is certain is that over a six month period in 1988, the four musicians came together and started rehearsing under the utterly bland moniker of Seymour, the name of one of Damon's fictitious characters. Within a month, Damon had written a track called 'She's So High' and their name was plastered all over London's tube trains. Over the next few months, Seymour began gigging sporadically in and around the capital, frequenting the dingy clubs that have produced so much talent over the years.

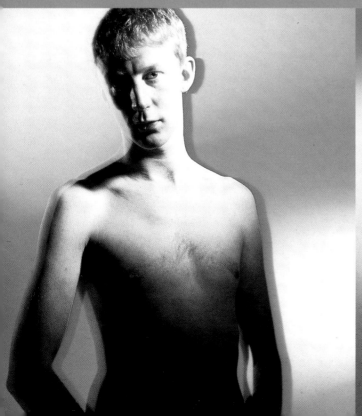

They sent a tape to Andy Ross, the ex-*Sounds* journalist who was now the supremo of Food Records, a nascent off-shoot of EMI. He tried to see Seymour but was refused entrance to Dingwall's Club in Camden. The same week there was a favourable review in the industry trade paper *Music Week* but they were listed as Feymour. It wasn't until four weeks later at The Powerhaus in Islington that Ross finally got to see them and he was impressed. Tape and gig convinced Ross that Seymour had potential. "It showed they had a clear grasp of the facets of songwriting," he said. "Everything was in its right place and in the right proportion." Of the demo tracks, two stuck in his mind ('She's So High' and 'Fool') while the other two were dismissed as art school rubbish (which they were).

Even so, this was enough for Ross to open his cheque book, and popular rumour suggests that Blur played only ten gigs before signing to Food Records. Within months they had £3,000 to record their first single, largely off the strength of 'She's So High'. Before they could get their hands on the cash though, Ross and his partner Dave Balfe (ex-Teardrop Explodes) demanded that they change their name. Several alternatives were offered, including The Shining Path, Sub, Whirlpool and Sensitise, but they decided on Blur. One final contractual detail demanded that drummer Dave would never play a gig in his traditional pyjama bottoms again, which thankfully he never did. Graham and Alex's degrees were left uncompleted as the newly-named band headed for their first gig as Blur.

Ross and Balfe felt that Blur had too many second hand sounds in their set and were not yet ready to record, so they sent the young group on a début tour in October 1990. It was brief, but useful, and after they returned Ross announced that the time was now right for their début single, 'She's So High', a track already established as a live favourite. It was a stunning début, punchy and bright with melancholic vocals and an infectious immediacy. Ross' instinct that this was the track to launch the band's career proved absolutely spot on – the single climbed to No. 48 in the national charts, impressive for an unknown act on an independent label. The band celebrated with a supporting 21-date UK tour and a Christmas date at Brixton Academy alongside The Soup Dragons. Suddenly, seemingly from nowhere, virtually overnight, Blur had arrived.

The speed of the band's ascent accelerated markedly when they released their second single 'There's No Other Way' in March 1991. It hit the Top 10, which meant another nationwide tour for the boys and general widespread acclaim. Alongside the musical success, the Blur boys found themselves being touted as pin-ups, with Damon's blue eyes finding their way onto thousands of poster bedecked bedroom walls. Their début, *Top Of The Pops* appearance was utterly shambolic and feverishly received. Children's morning TV slots followed, as did column after column in the teen press. At the same time, the more serious weekly music papers seemed confused by Blur's sudden arrival, yet more than happy to accommodate them in their pages as well. Even the tabloids joined in, ensuring mainstream recognition, with the *Daily Star* running a double page spread about the rumoured drinking binges and wild behaviour of the band, calling them 'Britain's Greatest Sex and Drugs Band'. One gig in Ipswich was filled with 1,000 screaming teenage girls; three nights later the band played the same set to 2,000 rockers in London's Town & Country Club. Blur it seemed, were flavour of the month.

The problem with being flavour of the month is that a month lasts only four weeks. In Blur's case, this was exacerbated because the massive success of 'There's No Other Way' was due not to the track alone but because it clung to the tail of the Madchester movement, a plethora of Manchester bands who revolutionised the rock and dance format, following in the tradition of Joy Division, New Order and lesser known acts like A Certain Ratio. The Stone Roses led the way with The Happy Mondays and Inspiral Carpets following closely behind, as 'baggy' music swept the nation up in a tide of flares, long sleeved shirts and Joe Bloggs clothing. The bands carried an apolitical, abstract apathy towards life which was reflected in their innovative music and served to heighten the appeal. 1989 was their year, although the repercussions for British music continued for some time after.

Blur arrived just as Madchester was thriving, and their second single was seen by more astute critics as too derivative, perhaps even plagiarised (with The Stone Roses' 'I Am The Resurrection' specified as the alleged original track). There *was* a startling similarity to much of the Manchester scene's sound, and The Stone Roses in particular, with the psychedelic guitars, Hammond riffing, and loping rhythms. Indeed, some confused 'There's No Other Way' as The Stone Roses' next single. The snatch of perfect post-baggy pop launched Blur into the headlines but threatened to destroy them just as quickly and effectively.

For now, the spotlight was theirs. During the summer of 1991, Blur joined a group of feted bands who were treated by the serious music press as the next big thing, and comically dubbed 'The Scene That Celebrates Itself'. Alongside Blur were single name bands such as Ride, Lush and Moose, and the unofficial scene became a cliquey indie drinking club, with the Syndrome Club on Oxford Street as its heart. Very soon, Blur's social antics had earned them the reputation of serious gadabouts in London. Ironically, 'the scene that celebrates itself' became known for bands who had little or nothing to say, lyrically or otherwise, which was amusing considering Blur's later media profile and lyrical slant. Blur enjoyed the attention and released their third single, 'Bang', in July 1991 when this artificial scene was at its peak. Even though the track was lacklustre compared to its predecessors (with a B-side that was far superior to the lead tune), the band continued to court and be courted by the press.

The reaction to their début album 'Leisure' in August 1991 was mixed, although for the most part it was positive. With most tracks produced by Stephen Street, the album was an interesting collection, but tended towards the derivative, with Blur too often letting their influences take priority over their own ideas. Graham was into the thrash atmospherics of Dinosaur Jr. and My Bloody Valentine, and this gave the record an overall noise tone that did not benefit their material, with 'Slow Down' the worst example of noise overkill throttling what was otherwise a decent song. The success of their first two singles, and to a lesser degree 'Bang' as well, made the haphazard remainder of the album something of a let-down, with only 'Repetition', the odd 'Sing' and the lurching 'Birthday' coming up to scratch.

Soon after its release, Graham himself referred to this album as Blur's 'indie detox album' where they exorcised all their Dinosaur Jr, MBV and C86 ghosts. Blur's followers did not agree – the tour to promote the album was ecstatically received, and the band spent most of the autumn and early winter playing to packed halls nationwide. Their success stretched as far as France where they were invited to play two large shows, while back home they stole the party from Jesus Jones at the Food Christmas Party gig at Brixton Academy. With all this interest, and the band's frenetic live shows developing all the time, and despite its average standard, 'Leisure' reached No.7 in the charts, a considerable success for the young band. This should have cemented their position as one of the bright young hopes of British pop.

Reality, however, was very different. The timing of 'Leisure' could not have been worse. Madchester was in its death throes, devoid of innovation and its two major proponents, The Stone Roses and The Happy Mondays, were involved in courtroom battles or drug abuse or both. Already the mainstream had begun to re-read the genre and sanitise it, and for many Blur were the major instigators of this. Their clichéd reproduction of the sound on 'There's No Other Way' was seen by many as a symbolic funeral march for Madchester. In 1992, in the *NME*, Graham said of their then-best known single: "'There's No Other Way' is a monumentally bland record, it's so banal, and that led to it being scrutinised, when in fact it meant absolutely nothing." Blur were now in grave danger of epitomising a dying breed, and being the runt of the litter too.

This was unfair. 'Leisure' for all its failings was not purely 'baggy' and the band were clearly not just a lolloping, post-ecstasy guitar outfit. Unfortunately, in the rush to blame someone for baggy's death, Blur's flashes of Syd Barrett quirkiness and their punk spirit were ignored. Against this was the fact that much of the album *did* resemble Madchester sounds, and the lyrical descriptions of youthful hedonism and epicurean lifestyles *did* mirror the ecstasy-riddled scene around baggy. Justifiable or not, Blur found themselves earmarked as the nation's scapegoats for a spent musical force, and the future looked gloomy.

Nothing was heard of the band until March 1992, by which time baggy had finally died. Even so, both the band and Food Records were confident that with their next single, 'Popscene', Blur could sweep aside all the derisory comments and criticisms of band wagon jumping. It was easy to see why they were so confident – 'Popscene' was a bristling and joyous track, light years away from both 'the scene that celebrates itself' (or shoe-gazing) and 'baggy'. It was a frantic, horn-laden mix of speeding guitars and thumping, swirling rock. Coinciding with this release, the band hitched a ride on the prestigious Rollercoaster tour led by The Jesus & Mary Chain, the British answer to the enormously successful Lollapalooza tour in the USA. Blur were delighted to join the tour, and play alongside Dinosaur Jr, Jesus & Mary Chain, and My Bloody Valentine. Ironically, the tour was the start of a catalogue of disasters that was to plague Blur over the next 12 months and almost destroy them.

First of all, the single bombed completely. 'Popscene' was a big departure from previous releases, and a very English sounding record, but it annoyed many people. Sales dipped quickly and it stalled at only No.32 after a slating from the bloodthirsty press. For the first single after a Top 10 album, and a good single at that, this was a major shock. Andy Ross at Food, and the band, were devastated. They had a follow up prepared for a few months after the release of 'Popscene' (a track called 'Never Clever' which eventually surfaced as a B-side) and dates pencilled in, all of which were abandoned. Press criticism was vicious and unforgiving, live dates failed to sell out (with the exception of a handful of great shows in Japan) and Blur saw themselves assigned to the 'whatever happened to' bracket.

The prestigious Rollercoaster tour proved to be a mixed blessing. While the band performed well and response was good, the tour itself was seen as the definitive 'shoe-gazing' tour, and this did not help a band desperate to throw off the shackles of media labelling. Much to their amazement, Blur soon realised it would probably have been better not to have been on the tour at all.

Thirdly, the music business was witnessing a new post-baggy order taking shape, led by Suede, who were sweeping aside the old guard. The Bowie/Roxy Music taste of Brett Anderson's Suede was anathema to Blur. 'Suede fever' was in full flow, with the *Melody Maker*'s now famous headline "The Best New Band In Britain" featuring Suede in an exact replica of the now-defunct *Sounds* magazine front cover headline with Blur. For a band as confident as Blur this was a severe blow. On top of this, Suede's own London landscape appeared to be a direct steal of the imagery with which Damon was toying. In addition, Damon's girlfriend Justine Frischmann was a previous member of Suede – some said she even thought of the name – and worse still, she was a previous girlfriend of the enigmatic and arrogant Anderson, whom Damon quickly came to see as the perpetrator of his band's troubles. He referred to Suede in interviews as 'the 's' word'. The Suede factor continued to gnaw at Blur's self-esteem and career from hereon in.

Fourthly, and perhaps most worryingly of all, Blur themselves were set on self-destruct. Their drinking increased, the live shows suffered and the band were quoted in the music press criticising all and sundry who dared to usurp their position. Instead of challenging the newcomers, Blur were disqualifying themselves from the race. The most blatant example of this was their disastrous tour of America, when they were on the very brink of collapse. The opening night saw crowd riots, fights with security, power cuts, and a dramatic escape through a backstage window and screeching off into the night with the security angrily chasing after them. With a ridiculous 44 dates to play and only three days off in two months, they drank their way around America, and the results were catastrophic. Band morale was at an all-time low.

Matters worsened when they returned home. Suede smiled up at them from every news-stand and stories of their American escapades had filtered home to reinforce the opinion that Blur was a spent force. Even Glastonbury in 1992 was a jaded and tired show. Then the new sessions for the next album went disastrously wrong – Dave Balfe insisted on using Andy Partridge of XTC as producer, but the band had hated the results (which included a cover of Buggles' 'Video Killed The Radio Star') even though Partridge himself got on with the band. They refused to use the fruitless sessions at all, and expressed their distaste by drinking heavily throughout the recording. Food blew their top at the waste. Moods darkened.

Then they discovered that virtually all of the royalties from their successful début album had vanished, and they were as good as bankrupt. Legal threats flew from lawyer to lawyer and tax problems loomed. They had been taken for a ride by the people closest to them. Even their own people were digging the boot in.

Amazingly, despite all this, Blur were still asked to headline the 'Gimme Shelter' gig at London's Town & Country Club in aid of homeless people on the streets of the capital. Opening the show were Suede. Against the backdrop of months of disaster, Blur were in a foul mood and drank non-stop all day. By the time of the show, they were plastered. Oblivious to the fact that Suede had earlier performed a wildly received blistering set, Blur stumbled on stage incapable of producing the kind of live show for which they were well known. Damon staggered up to the microphone and said "It's gonna be shit tonight, so fuck off". He was right – it was shit. Damon made matters worse by hitting a bouncer with his microphone and falling about uselessly. Blur were hopeless, a drunken, unprofessional failure. Suede left the venue surrounded by the music press and soon after were reviewed in hallowed terms. Blur left alone and pissed, sneered at with derision and scorn. Carry On Punk some people called it. Others wondered if Blur could even do that, and if this had been the last ever Blur gig.

The following day, Dave Balfe took a hung-over and bedraggled Damon out to lunch, where he told him that in his opinion Blur were as good as finished. They were spending record company money as if it was going out of fashion. Their attitude was appalling and they hadn't produced any decent new material for months. They seemed obsessed with the Suede factor, and with back-biting other bands at every turn. They seemed bitter, twisted and unmotivated. Balfe told Damon how the same problems had destroyed The Teardrop Explodes. He talked of the need to change and sort things out. At the end of the lunch, he gave Blur an ultimatum: you have one month to sort this mess out or it's all over.

Damon told the band what had happened. It was now or never and the ultimatum inspired their first and only band rule – there would be no more drinking before concerts ever again (it was a rule Graham had to adhere to - his doctor had ordered him to lay off alcohol shortly before to avoid serious health problems). Then they slowly started to write again. With just the four of them in a studio in Fulham, with no press favours, no money, no interest other than their own, and very nearly no record deal, Blur started to write their next album. The title was quickly decided upon, and could not have been more appropriate: 'Modern Life Is Rubbish'.

Such was the attitude towards Blur that when 'Modern Life Is Rubbish' was released in May 1993, the press remained wary of the band they had never quite understood anyway. When they heard the album and saw the accompanying new look, there were even more raised eyebrows. Shock horror – Blur, the unshaven, beer boys of post-baggy failure had re-invented themselves. Press manipulation and contrivance were the words on everyone's lips. If Blur were to re-establish themselves, they had their work cut out.

In fact, they were more than up to the task. Clues to the new record could have been garnered from the one-off New Year gig at the Fulham Hibernian, where they were supported by the Salvation Army band and the fashionable but soon to be redundant Huggy Bear (at this gig a select number of free one-sided copies of a track called 'The Wassail Song' were given away to lucky punters). The album itself was leagues ahead of their début, and proved that the dire experiences of 1992 had been cathartic and creatively very productive. Returning to the studio in the autumn of 1992 after the failed Andy Partridge sessions, they re-established an excellent working relationship with Stephen Street who had been at the controls for most of 'Leisure', and had since produced much of Morrissey's solo work. The recordings went well, although Dave Balfe sent Damon back to write two more songs when he presented the finished album to Food (Damon wrote 'For Tomorrow' and 'Chemical World' that day).

At its core, the album reflected on their recent adverse experiences and offered at the same time an affectionate vignette of English life in an honourable tradition that went back to the Sixties. For the first time, this peculiar English fascination surfaced with conspicuous clarity, and in many senses was the key element of the record. Because their third album, with its similar Anglo-centric focus, seems in hindsight to have been a guaranteed success, it is easy to forget that in 1992 grunge and all things American were the rage, with shabby clothes, long hair and multi-decibel distortion attracting record companies wielding cheque books. Blur proved to be awkward and stubbornly different. Many people laughed at the English focus of 'Modern Life' but Damon had no interest in America's teenage wasteland or most of its music – the working title for the album had even been 'England *vs* America'.

The majority of the band's reference points were classic English pop, Madness, The Kinks and The Jam. While the town on everybody's lips was Seattle, Damon chose London: Primrose Hill, Portobello Road and the Underground. Cramming his lyrics with unfashionable names, a language that was distinctly 'un-pop', was exactly what he wanted, as he told the press in 1993: "Writing about England hadn't been done since Madness, everyone said we'd write ourselves into obscurity. I thought it was obvious that the press and the public would get fed up with America. We were ahead of the game by a year." Damon's confidence was such that he even went as far as to say that 'Modern Life Is Rubbish' "is the most significant comment on popular culture since 'Anarchy in the UK'."

'Modern Life' was delivered in a sound that was uniquely British. The songs were more structured and more clever than before, with a vague narrative that described a host of people, places and relationships, all of them very English. The Peeping Toms, commuters and petrol smells of London suggested a concept, and signified that Blur were willing to write about things other bands ignored. The retrogressive tendencies were still there, as with the immediate but rather weak 'For Tomorrow', but the band appeared to be more in control, more focused and more original this time around. There were two real gems in 'Advert' and 'Star-Shaped', and there was variety, with pub knees-ups ('Intermission'), pure pop (the throbbing 'Sunday Sunday') and acoustic ballads ('Blue Jeans'). There were snatches of Bowie mixed with odd Seventies production, a definite penchant for fairground tunes, and stories of Damon's own fictitious characters, such as the 'modern day retard' Colin Zeal, who lives in a new town in Essex. It was an annoyingly different record, unfashionable, unpalatable even, but with enough eccentricity and imaginative individualism to make it an admirable release. Blur were back.

The new sound and lyrical focus was accompanied by a new look, a sharper, streetwise style. Sharp suits and Doc boots, short hair and turned-up jeans, contrasted sharply with the grunge look of saggy jumpers and long greasy hair. When the album came out in May 1993, it could not have been more different from the shortly-to-be released third album by Nirvana which everyone was talking about. The lead-in single 'For Tomorrow', released in April, sold well, reaching No.28 and earning public acclaim from Paul Weller. With the papers warming to Blur, the album release was preceded by the slogan 'modern life is rubbish' appearing all across London. Most of it was sprayed by the band themselves, including one large graffiti on Clacton seafront which so enraged the Colchester evening paper that there was a temporary ban on Blur coverage. Their cause was not helped when Dave was involved in a drunken punch-up with the new Buzzcocks bassist, but thankfully this was the exception. 'Modern Life Is Rubbish' was to re-invent Blur.

1993 was the year that Blur cut loose from the damaging preconceptions that baggy and all its early antics had laid on them, and at Reading Festival's second stage, where they were headliners, the whole new feel clicked brilliantly together in a storming set. While Matt Johnson's The The were boring everyone on the main stage, Blur played a blinder of a set and stole the weekend for themselves. From here on, Blur's live reputation built and built and became a mainstay for their future success.

Ironically, it seemed as if the 'Gimme Shelter' concert, which had appeared to be their nadir, had actually shown a more honest side to the band, and was a crucial watershed in their career. If they needed any reminding of how close they had come to imploding, they had only to watch their own 'Star-Shaped' long form video which was released in 1993, featuring three years of footage on the road with Blur. It was a catalogue of hedonism that the video package itself described as "candid camera on the road with Blur, from Reading 1991, through the dark ages of the EEC in 1992 and then on to Modern Life". Vomit and sickness are everywhere, with drunken, staggering band members appearing every five minutes to demonstrate the degree to which the terrible events of 1992 had left Blur reeling. Even the great John Peel seemed reserved about the band, calling them 'dangerous hits of melody.' 'Star-Shaped' confirmed their erstwhile reputation as serious lager louts. The most obviously poignant moment in the film comes when Damon is asked 'What was it like to be in Blur in 1992?' and all that follows is total silence, four friends unable to articulate how pointless, destructive and wearing the whole year had been. 'Star Shaped' was a testament to Blur's 'stickability' and a reminder to them what they had come through. With 'Modern Life Is Rubbish' under their belts it was clear they had no intention of going back.

The July tour to support this album was highly successful, and marked the first diversion Blur had used from a bare stage. This time, they performed alongside a TV, a sofa, and a variety of household appliances on a set that reflected their clear fascination with all things mundane and urbane. Not that the live show needed any artificial help – with band spirits high, the gigs for the national album tour pricked many ears and turned heads back to what Blur were doing, and those expecting The Kinks or The Jam were surprised by the much harder live sound, more like The Clash or The Sex Pistols. It was followed by a headline slot on the *Melody Maker* 'Sugary Tea' tour in October, clear indication of just how far Blur had gone towards pulling their fate out of the fire. At one stage in 1992 they were universally despised, and now they were popular headliners again.

In three cities – Newcastle, Coventry and Brighton – they were asked to hold a series of debates with fans, during which all manner of questions were posed; about the music, their lifestyles and also the possible racist suggestions of some of Blur's imagery. With Morrissey parading around Finsbury Park draped in a Union Jack before a crowd with a large skinhead contingent, the abuse and manipulation of British patriotism for seedy motives was very topical. Blur were clearly not remotely interested in this angle and replied very confidently that there was no need to worry. "We're not crazed patriots. I'm just not ashamed of using what I've grown up with as a creative aid," Damon told *Melody Maker*. Asked how he would like Blur to be seen in retrospect, Damon replied: "We're arrogant enough to think we could stand as a mirror of the culture of our time. But we'll probably be remembered for something silly and inconsequential, because that's the random nature of things."

The second single from 'Modern Life' was the bland 'Chemical World' with its rather blatant mixture of Madness *circa* 'Our House' and Mott The Hoople, but it still sold well and furthered Blur's growing rejuvenation. The process continued with the much better third single, 'Sunday Sunday', which was released in October, shortly after the superb Reading performance, and to coincide with the storming 'Sugary Tea' dates. By now, Blur were back on the front covers and band morale was again sky high. On tour Damon scribbled away and by the end of these dates, in late October, much of the groundwork for their next album was completed. As soon as they returned home, they headed for the studio to begin the sessions, which many had thought they would never see. By March 1994 it was ready, and its release was heralded by the success of the band in the music media end of year polls for 1993. In the *Melody Maker* Readers' Polls, Blur won the Best Live Act category, as well as coming second in the Best Band and Third in Best LP sections. The world was prepared to listen to Blur again. Anticipation for the third album was high. Would Blur have anything worth saying?

The Eiffel Tower. The Empire State Building. Walthamstow Dog Track. All have seen glamorous parties to launch albums, and it goes without saying that when Blur released 'Parklife', Paris and New York didn't enter the equation. The massed ranks of the music industry, and not a few stars – The Pet Shop Boys, Elastica, Carter, Pwei, Sleeper, Lush, Swervedriver, Eddie Izzard and even the great Eddie Tenpole Tudor – headed for the greyhound racing oval in E17 for the occasion. All went well, and many beers were sunk, until the band's sponsored race – Blur Parklife Stakes – came to be run. After a short half lap, the rabbit exploded and two of the dogs went for each other's throats. The race was void. Any other band might have taken this as a bad omen for the forthcoming album; not Blur, because they knew they had produced a blinder.

The first single from the new record, the infectious 'Girls And Boys', came in March, and smashed into the Top 5. Based on the sex and sangria image of Club 18-30 holidays, it was quirky, niggly, catchy pop at its best, with a tinny drum machine and bleeping backdrop. It was Blur's most audacious record to date and was quite rightly hailed as a mini classic. The only question was, could Blur reproduce this sort of form over an entire album?

Having dismissed the working titles of 'Soft Porn' or 'Sport', the band opted for 'Parklife', released in April 1994. It was greeted with wild universal acclaim, critical awards, and a year's worth of intense media frenzy. Blur had achieved what had seemed unthinkable just two short years before. Characterised by the sounds, sights and smells of all things English, and more particularly London, 'Parklife' was peopled by oddball characters, woven into a rich tapestry of intrigue and detail. Dead-pan irony accompanied the sentimental kitsch of the weird and wonderful characters Damon had produced. Blur were inviting us to be voyeurs, spying through the keyhole of our own lives.

There was 'Tracy Jacks', a song about the behind-closed-door perversions of a lower middle class forty-something transvestite, followed by 'End Of A Century', a sad lament that Damon now maintains is his favourite Blur song. Then there's 'Parklife' itself, with vocals by the actor Phil Daniels, who starred as Jimmy in the 1979 film *Quadrophenia*, made at the height of the late Seventies Mod revival. The soundtrack was based on the 1974 album by The Who, and featured the Brighton Mod/Rocker clashes of 10 years before.

And so the album went on, with Mod singalongs, rinky dink instrumentals and ballads in a bizarre yet brilliant collection of ideas and sounds. There were several instrumental segues, done with enough style to give the record a certain cinematic quality. Mellow grandiose tracks sat next to plain pop; there was no real flow, with each track crashing into the next, sometimes abrasively and awkwardly, but if it was a mess, it was a bloody appealing one. Although there were similarities, this album was far more focused than Blur's previous records. The only blemish was 'Trouble In The Message Centre', which, musical terminology aside, was crap second-hand Gary Newman.

This album marked out Blur's individualism. No other group had succeeded in articulating exactly what they were about with such clarity. Urban living was the key and the core, and no-one else was writing about this. Damon also made it quite clear that theirs was not an unreserved admiration for all things English, when he told the *NME* in June: "All my songs criticise this country. They're all about characters who are fed up and are trying to get away." The band's lyrical and musical presentation of this theme was varied and accomplished enough to carry the diversity on the record without becoming incohesive, and their tongue-in-cheek approach meant there was never any pomposity or pretension involved. The album was released the same month that Nirvana's Kurt Cobain tragically took his own life, at a time when many people were losing faith in music. Among the high praise for Blur, *NME* summed up most precisely what everyone else was thinking, when they reviewed the album and said "For once an LP that deserves to be played from start to finish... Blur have made what will undoubtedly be seen as the greatest pop album of 1994. It is easy to forget that albums can be this fabulous."

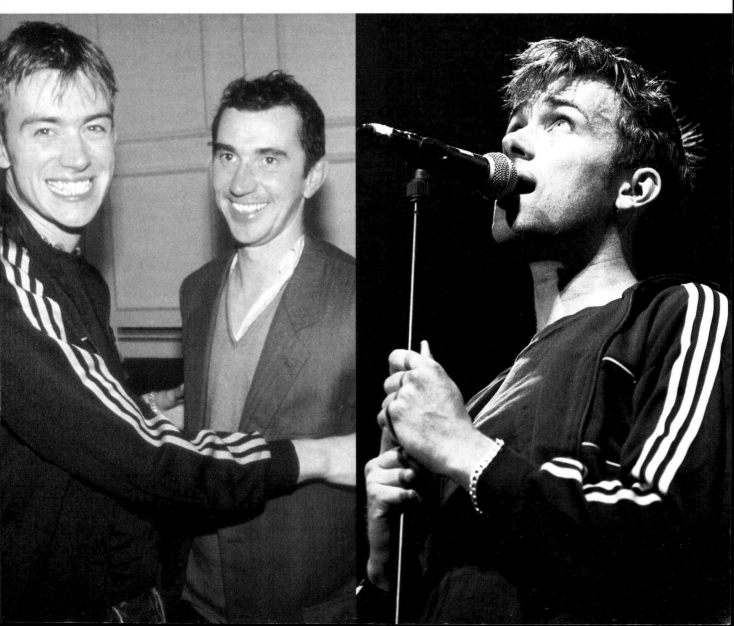

A new record called for a new look. The Doc Martens were gone, as were the sharp suits, now replaced by Puma trainers and fawn Harringtons. Fashionable labels such as Sergio Taccini and Ellesse were back, just as they had been for most people way back during the 'casual' days of the summer of 1984. Blur, again, looked different. Damon half-heartedly called it 'modual', a mix between mod and casual. The only element of the new image that was not universally accepted was the band's use of greyhounds on the album artwork. Although intended as a direct link to the idiosyncratic theme of the album, there was dissent from animal lovers. In a letter to the *Melody Maker* in November of 1994, one angry fan put it very directly: "Don't buy Blur – they sanction the killing of defenceless animals. This certainly doesn't endear Damon's cheeky grin to me."

Nevertheless, record sales were huge, with the album smashing into the charts at No.1, replacing the tired and over-inflated Pink Floyd, which was ironic considering that Blur had occasionally been compared to a Nineties Syd Barrett. In the six months after its release, it never once fell below No. 15, which was as high as 'Modern Life' ever reached. The subsequent singles from the album, 'Girls And Boys', 'To The End' and 'Parklife', sold heavily, with *Top Of The Pops* appearances for all, and more album sales as a spin-off. By the end of the summer of 1994, 'Parklife' was already the year's most talked about record.

Damon and the band certainly had lots of talking to do – the media couldn't get enough of them. In the countless features that followed the album's release, Damon's half-baked theories of 'the travels of the mystical lager eaters' reflected the opium eaters of 19th century Thomas De Quincy, but he didn't want to be seen as the struggling artist: "I can't stand the idea of being a lonely sad bedsit poet. I'd much rather be perceived as loud and arrogant, because all our sensitivity is in our records." He also went on to say… "If the British music industry wants a big band again they've got to back Blur in a big way, because we aren't going to implode" and finished off by stating proudly "yes, we are the best group in Britain and, yes, we probably are the best British group since The Smiths."

The dates for the tour, their first full scale outing since the shock of returning home to find their début album royalties had been stolen, were sold out well in advance. At London's Alexandra Palace in October, a venue that hadn't heard the sound of an angry electric guitar since the days of Morrissey and The Stone Roses, fans were given bingo cards as they entered the huge arena. They were treated to an excellent bill, including Supergrass, Corduroy and Pulp. Then there was an intermission, with ice cream and chocolates, before a bingo caller walked on stage and announced that the winner of the competition would win 'a night out with Blur'. By the time he had read out the numbers there were 8,000 winners, and Blur duly obliged them all by strolling on stage, bedecked with pink lampshades.

The crowd began to pogo wildly from the first note of 'Tracy Jacks'. Alex coolly brooded over his bass, a fag permanently dangling from the corner of his shy face. Graham crouched over his guitar like a craftsman, while Dave thumped away at the back. Damon was in his usual confident mood, striding across the stage, bouncing along and chatting casually to the crowd, occasionally laughing at words to his own songs. For 'Badhead' and 'End Of A Century' the band introduced a brass section, which complemented the already full sound, and they even made a few concessions to the past with brilliant renditions of 'There's No Other Way' and 'She's So High'. The set comprised electro beats, angelic harmonies, jittery melodies and buzzsaw guitar, all topped off with Damon's heartfelt lyrical insight. The biggest roar of the night was reserved for the appearance ("for the last time ever") of Phil Daniels on 'Parklife', whereupon 8,000 fans repeated the wild reception the band received when they had headlined in front of 100,000 at the Glastonbury festival during the summer.

In October, Blur played a nine-date city hop in America, but the work ethic that is now obligatory for genuine success in America is not part of Blur's style. While The Cranberries played over 100 US gigs in one year – and sold a million albums as a result – Blur reduced the number of gigs by 33 and remained content with the success in the UK, seeing any positive reaction in America as a bonus. The shows were all sold out weeks in advance despite their well-documented dislike of American culture, but fans in the country which had until now proved to be the band's nemesis failed to see the arch-irony of 'Magic America'. Blur just played the songs, ignored the Mod parkas and Lambrettas parked outside and smiled cheekily. During the American tour the band wrote about 15 tracks which will make up the majority of the next album, the third in the 'life' trilogy, which is due for release in August 1995. As Damon told *NME*, Blur are not bogged down by the so-called mysteries of the rock and roll business: "The thing you've got to understand about Blur is that there's not an ounce of rock'n'roll in us. That's why we're capable of making an album a year, instead of waiting around with the amps turned on waiting for the vibes."

A smaller scale jaunt around Japan brought further rewards, by which time Blur were christened the Modfathers of a new Mod revival. The clothes and the British angle were cited as evidence, but Blur were never really Mod, just Mod icons. There were Mod images in their work – the parka in the video of 'For Tomorrow' and the post-speed binge lad sprawled on a Mod target bedspread for the cover of the 'Star-Shaped' video, à la Jimmy in Quadrophenia. The band rightly avoided any great involvement in this suggestion.

With such acclaim, it was inevitable that Blur would feature heavily in the year's music industry awards, but no-one could have foreseen just how successful they were. In effect, they swept the boards. Although they missed out at the Mercury Awards to the dance retrogression of M People, the newly prestigious Brit Awards were a different matter. They collected a record four awards, one more than the previous best by Seal in 1992. Trophies for Best Band, accompanied their three others for Best Single, Best Video and Best Album. At the ceremony, Damon acknowledged Oasis, the new pretenders to the Blur crown, and suggested the Best Album award should have been a joint one. During the show, the artist formerly known as Prince, now universally called Squiggle, wrote 'SLAVE' on his face in protest at what he saw as restrictive practices by his record company, which had limited his income to 'only' several millions of dollars. Later in the evening, Dave Rowntree raised a chuckle by turning up for one of Blur's awards with 'DAVE' written on his cheek, and it was still there the following week, when Blur appeared on *Top Of The Pops*.

The success of 'Parklife' had other fascinating repercussions. Damon presented *Top Of The Pops* himself, and had an orchestral score for the album submitted by an 'A' level student at a sixth form college where they played a secret gig which was recorded by Radio 4's *Kaleidoscope*. Much to their delight, *The Sun* ran a 'Ten Things You Didn't Know About Blur' column, in which it was alleged that one of their habits was 'stripping naked for weird male-bonding sessions'. By now, Damon was a fully fledged sex god in the press, although his girlfriend, Justine from Elastica, told *Smash Hits* magazine: "He has one of the lowest sex drives of any boy I've ever met. He's not that into sex." Damon fuelled this view by saying he'd always thought he was cool until he saw a video of a live show and admitted he was in fact a clown and a geek. There was even a Spitting Image take on 'Parklife' about the trials of the Royal family entitled 'Charles Life'. More seriously, Blur also won four of the Brat Awards, those given out by the *NME*, and important in so much as they acknowledged those bands who were at the forefront of alternative British music. Ironic really: *NME* wouldn't even spit on Blur two years ago.

The huge success of 'Parklife' marked the culmination of four years of Blur being awkward, different and difficult, a band no-one quite knew what to do with. After the drip-dry baggy beginnings of 'Leisure', the band seemed to focus on everything that was unfashionable and unpopular. When grunge and America were in favour, Blur pitched their tent in an English oasis, wearing tight jeans, Doc Martens and sharp suits. When the Mod look caught on, they lost the boots and dressed casual again. With Britain largely derided as a spent force, Blur praised its vibrant culture and highlighted its pitfalls. Grunge signalled the death of British pop and Blur resurrected it. Lyrically and musically, they have consistently ignored trends and instead highlighted the absurd nature of ordinary English life. In the same way their flawed first album killed off baggy, their superb third album killed off grunge, but for very different reasons. They went out on a limb to pursue an unfashionable English vision which may explain why they were occasionally arrogant when 'Parklife' eventually roared into life. Through sheer self-belief and perseverance, Blur captured an audience that spans several generations of rock kids, indie girls, ravers and rockers, nostalgists, futurists, thirty-somethings and teeny boppers, music lovers of almost every creed.

Despite the critics constantly referring Blur's achievements back to The Kinks, The Jam, Madness and other great British bands, the comparisons are irrelevant. Blur take what they like and produce something fresh and new from that, and nostalgia plays very little part. Damon himself cites classical music, and Brecht and Weill in particular, as his biggest influence. Indeed, most of Blur were too young even to be bogged down by punk. The similarities are there of course, and they do use the styles and hues of classical British songwriting to reflect the present national mood. However, the band are all too young to have studied these sources first-hand, and their re-readings are fresh and new. Let Blur bask in their own glory, rather than the reflected spotlight of someone else.

After their career went from bad to worse and youthful hedonism took its toll, they plunged through crisis after crisis, ending 1992 as a spent force, drunken, unloved and penniless. By re-inventing themselves for the defensive 'Modern Life', Blur breathed new life into their weary bones, and adopted a stance that was as brave as it was individual. Throughout their career, they have managed to produce a steady stream of quirky pop songs, from the early baggy pastiche to the finest moments of 'Parklife'. With the enormous success of that eclectic and wide reaching third album, their trials and tribulations have come to an end, and Damon's prophetic words back in 1990 have been proved correct – they are now established as the quintessential British pop band of the Nineties.

discography

singles

She's So High (edit) / I Know
Food FOOD 26 (7")
November 1990

She's So High (Definitive) / Sing / I Know
Food 12FOOD (12")
November 1990

She's So High / I Know (extended) / Down
Food CDFOOD 26 (CD)
November 1990

There's No Other Way / Inertia
Food FOOD 29 (7")
May 1991

There's No Other Way (extended) / Inertia /
Mr Briggs / I'm All Over
Food 12FOOD 29 (12")
May 1991

There's No Other Way (Blur Remix) /
Won't Do It / Day Upon Day (live)
Food 12FOODX 29 (12")
May 1991

Bang / Luminous
Food FOOD 31 (7")
July 1991

Bang (extended) / Explain / Luminous / Uncle Love
Food 12FOOD 31 (12")
July 1991

Bang / Explain / Luminous / Berserk
Food CDFOOD 31 (CD)
July 1991

High Cool (Easy Listening Mix) / Bad Day (Remix)
Food 12BLUR 4 (12" Promo only)
July 1991

Popscene / Mace
Food FOOD 37 (7")
March 1992

Popscene / I'm Fine / Mace / Garden Central
Food 12FOOD 37 (12")
March 1992

Popscene / Mace / Badgeman Brown
Food CDFOOD 37 (CD)
March 1992

The Wassail Song
Food BLUR 6 (7")
Given away free at 1992 Christmas show

For Tomorrow / Into Another / Hanging / Peach
Food 12FOOD 40 (12")
April 1993

For Tomorrow (Visit To Primrose Hill extended) /
Peach / Bone Bag
Food CDFOOD 40 (CD)
April 1993

For Tomorrow (single version) / When The Cows Come
Home / Beachcomber / For Tomorrow (acoustic version)
Food CDSFOOD 40 (CD)
April 1993

Chemical World / Maggie May
Food FOOD 45 (7" red vinyl)
June 1993

Chemical World / Never Clever (live) / Pressure On Julian
(live) / Come Together (live)
Food CDFOODS 45 (CD)
June 1993

Chemical World / Young And Lively / Es Smecht / My Ark
Food CDSFOOD 45 (CD)
June 1993

Sunday Sunday / Tell Me Tell Me
Food FOODS 46 (7" yellow vinyl)
October 1993

Sunday Sunday / Long Legged / Mixed Up
Food 12FOODS 46 (12")
October 1993

Sunday Sunday / Dizzy / Fried / Shimmer
Food CDFOODS 46 (CD)
October 1993

Sunday Sunday / Daisy Bell / Let's All Go Down The Strand
Food CDFOODX 46 (CD)
October 1993

Girls And Boys / Magpie / People In Europe
Food FOODS 47 (7")
February 1994

Girls And Boys / Magpie / Anniversary Waltz
Food CDFOODS 47 (CD)
February 1994

Girls And Boys / People In Europe / Peter Panic
Food CDFOODX 47 (CD)
February 1994

To The End / Girls And Boys (Pet Shop Boys 7" remix) /
Girls And Boys (Pet Shop Boys 12" remix)
Food 12FOOD 50 (12")
May 1994

To The End / Threadneedle Street / Got Yer
Food CDFOOD 50 (CD)
May 1994

Parklife / Super Shopper
Food FOOD LH 53 (7")
September 1994

Parklife / Super Shopper /
To The End (French version) / Beard
Food 12FOOD 53 (12")
September 1994

Parklife / Beard / To The End (French version)
Food CDFOOD 53 (CD)
September 1994

Parklife / Super Shopper / Theme From An Imaginary Film
Food CDFOODS 53 (CD)
September 1994

Parklife / Super Shopper / Theme From An Imaginary Film
Food CDFOODDJ 53 (Promo CD)
September 1994

albums

LEISURE
She's So High / Bang / Slow Down / Repetition /
Bad Day / Sing / There's No Other Way / Fool /
Come Together / High Cool / Birthday /
Wear Me Down
Food FOOLP 6 / Food FOODCD 6
August 1991

MODERN LIFE IS RUBBISH
For Tomorrow / Advert / Colin Zeal / Pressure On
Julian / Star Shaped / Blue Jeans / Chemical World /
Sunday Sunday / Olly Water / Miss America /
Villa Rosie / Coping / Turn It Up / Resigned
Food FOOLP9 / Food FOODCD 9
May 1993

PARKLIFE
Girls And Boys / Tracy Jacks / End Of A Century /
Parklife / Bank Holiday / Badhead / The Debt Collector /
Far Out / To The End / London Loves / Trouble In The
Message Centre / Clover Over Dover / Magic America /
Jubilee / This Is A Low / Lot 105
Food FOOLP 10 / Food COODCD 10
April 1994

miscellaneous

Food Christmas Party 1991: Resigned (demo) /
High Cool (Easy Listening mix)
Food TCFOOD 34 (cassette only) Various artists compilation,
given away free at Food's 1991 Christmas party

In A Field Of Their Own – Glastonbury '92:
Sunday Sunday (live)
NME GLASTON 1 DCD (Various artists compilation CD)
September 1992

Ruby Trax: Maggie May
NME 40 CD (Various artists compilation CD)
October 1992

Five Alone Take 2: Advert
(Mark Goodier session version)

MMMC 2 (cassette only) Melody Maker various artists compilation,
given away free in October 1993

Peace Together: Oliver's Army
Island CID 8018/518 063-2 (Various artists compilation CD)
June 1993

Who Covers Who: Substitute
CM Discs CM 006 (Various artists compilation CD of Who covers)
1993

Great Expectations: For Tomorrow (live)
XFM CD1 (Various artists compilation CD)
July 1993